RESISTANCE
COLIN CAMPBELL ROBINSON

Newton-le-Willows

Published in the United Kingdom in 2025
by The Knives Forks And Spoons Press,
51 Pipit Avenue,
Newton-le-Willows,
Merseyside,
WA12 9RG.

ISBN 978-1-916590-14-4

Copyright © Colin Campbell Robinson 2025.

The right of Colin Campbell Robinson to be identified as the author of this work has been asserted by them in accordance with the Copy rights, Designs and Patents Act of 1988. All rights reserved. No part of this publication may be reproduced, stored in a retrieval system, transmitted in any form or by any means, electronic, photocopying, recording or otherwise, without prior permission of the publisher.

Acknowledgements:

Resistance won the best unpublished poetry book at the Eyelands International Book Prize 2021.

An edited version of 'Resistant' was published in the *Declarations of Freedom* anthology issued by Scottish PEN 2020. Rene Char's poems, the 'Fragments of Heraclitus' and the 'Declaration of Arbroath', 1320, provided inspiration.

The poetry of Yannis Ritsos and in particular his last book, *Late into the Night*, provided background for 'The Night is Late'.

A Greek translation of 'The Night is Late' appeared in an e-book published by Strange Days in May 2022.

Josef Koudelka's book *Invasion 68 Prague* was the catalyst for 'Doors in Prague'.

Contents

Resistant   5
The Night is Late   21
Doors in Prague   33

Resistant

History is a long succession of words
leading to the same conclusions.
To contradict them is our duty.

— **Rene Char**

Prologue

Resistance, clarity; confusion, collaboration: The latter steals the day every day.

On their journey they wavered and baulked. Are there those who do otherwise? The sun does not beat them, they merely surrender.

Vile fluids introduced moment-to-moment, no longer a drip, more of a swollen flood.

From the boundless, we come, to be bound.

1.

In the dark the hunt is always on for us, we, the vanquished, the nearly vanished.

Midnight is the knell, noon the burning. All the other heavens are in-between. Pursuing light or darkness as if they are the same.

Noise drowns out all opportunities; we are engulfed by blare, every moment a farrago, a performance, a trial; then comes the judgement.

Miss the mark; bring on tragedy.

2.

In the present world we shrink the real, burn candles of tainted blood, sleep outside of slumber.

Something pervasive isn't noticed; the conjurers and their foolish fire.

Gloomy creator, yet the creation is both ambitious and expectant.

In faith we find no solace. From birth take deep breaths.

3.

They poisoned the well of being. Hope of recovery remains low. This is what the devil meant by a thousand years. An unwelcome diagnosis, a certain end; live as if these are the conditions. As always there's the question of pain; who suffers, who relieves?

Everywhere there is a slackness taking satisfaction in being slack. And faced with this intransigence resistance has no further option. What creates violence or more succinctly who?

Never forget when the time comes your neighbours, your shopkeepers can easily become hoodlums. The guilty slip passed the bar as they are want to do, they've now had ample time to destroy creation.

Harsh reprisals haunt the dim horizon.

4.

Without the shore's support don't trust the sea, the wind whispers.

Suffer the pain of intuition.

Flowing night-verse; wakefulness breaks exalted speech.

At the tether end, hurt by the rhythm in our hands, then, the flight.

The impossible is beyond attainment, yet, it is our guide-light.

5.

Is it possible to live a life with few enemies and what does it mean when you realise you have few enemies? Never having to confront someone holding your life in their hands, someone you have never met wielding a loaded gun.

The enemy is always certain when casting doubt. Foreboding, fear of potential trouble, always on the job.

A black car cruises up a dead end street: such commotion; such memories. Ambushed, buried alive, shot in the back; so many options available to the ruthless.

What will be their next move, always the question. Because they always know exactly where they are they claim they can never be lost. The wilful and the senseless conspire. Everything is forgotten with purpose.

Meanwhile in another country and in another and in another ad infinitum: the fall.

6.

Avoid the bee, the snake; shun venom and honey.

Sharp hawthorn blossom; his first alphabet.

Luxury is crime: the fountain sprang from the granite ground to tell him.

Dispirited words, rough relations, knuckle-bones cast by the hand of betrayal.

Who'll dare say what we've destroyed is worth a hundred times more than our dreams.

7.

Beyond this square, in the crematorium, the dead are debating our future. Don't expect generosity.

Word, storm, ice, and blood: four words coagulating as frost.

Speaking as if speech has finally lost all meaning. This has happened before.

All the world's a text and we merely send it.

The words run out quicker than the days.

8.

From the twin doors of the labyrinth emerge two passionate hands.

How can the end be justified by means?
There is no end, only means in perpetuity; always more machinations.

The bone-heap, a dynasty suffocating reflection: no art, no more. All is the grave.

Can hurt be dissolved by a steady heart?
By the way, the genie escapes suffering as he escapes everything.

9.

Endless change murmuring on the ruined pier: only if you choose to be on the ship Life-in-Death can you anchor here. The year of harrowing obligations still to come.

No more beds for the transient.

The odds against the evens divide and rule. Incalculable baseness; we are below each other's gaze, this is our fatal disposition.

Narrow nights follow wide days, no place in-between. Duplicity is as common as the dawn, ambiguous as dust.

According to St Genet there is only betrayal.

10.

Gods die from closeness. Keep an arms-length.

Only the musician dances like a devil licking the blues.

The book has been betrayed by life in the inferno of consumption and power.

Distant cloud, as seen by a steely gaze, is both sinuous and static.

If you don't accept what is offered, then, one day you will be beggars and your refusal will be great.

True clarity at the first step; breathe the breeze at the open door.

Clothe me in snow, tender heaven, make me drink your tears.

Start the journey, press on till evening, respect what the road says despite delays.

Accept the straw wishes of this earth transcribed by criss-crossing birds.

11.

Then, at sunrise, eyes open and the heart remembers. The time of struggle continues; we mean to stand. To act once, then twice with the same resolution is the aim.

To name someone an alchemist is the highest praise; iron turned to soul, nightmare to dream, freedom alone, in truth.

Falling through space, landing in time, the dove alights in peace. To feed birds from our hand is our destiny.

Sorrow is the final grain.

Notes

1. On his journey to Armenia he made some observations concerning the subtle acidic reactions of the eye and concluded it was an organ possessed of hearing.

2. His eye inclined more to singing than to speaking.

3. Years later he noted that exclusion and solitude are the destiny of those who compose, and, a lyrical response to the world is the studied and centred act of attention and meditation.

4. The silk handkerchiefs change colour as we watch, he says.

5. And of course we remember St Simone's words: Whenever we are closely attentive, we destroy some of the evil in ourselves.

6. Requiring attention and meditation, maybe experimentation in the woods near here, haunted as they are by the ancients.

7. There he is, the rascal of insecurity, he who fabricates the pointless.

8. Spring gleaning, glacier without end, are part of his spell-line.

9. Is it the dead who dine and the living who cry, eating only stones, he asks?

10. Today, facing the bleak, the tragic in the moment before, not after. Luminous vision, the eye listening, he takes his leave on a naked boat.

La Verre Galant
34 Blvd D'aguillon
Port Vauban

The night is late

So my friends, good-bye, and good luck.
Not one of night's stars is a lie.

– Yannis Ritsos

On crisp evenings they gather to plot the revolution of everyday, Yannis is among them. On their barstools they shift positions. Fortunately he and his chair are in complete agreement.

What is the proletarian moon, I ask? The moon that swells the ocean and floods our heart, he replies. We play these monochords in the timeless way. Line after line, breathing.

He claims to have been taught the world by his body. I believe him. Listen to your own pores.

Can the explanation be in the inexplicable? I can't explain. Always on foot, he says.

Late and dark, everyone has left the square; only Yannis remains, distractedly shining a shoe against his corduroy leg. A bird lands on a branch, sings about clouds.

What is the centre of the complete circle, I ask? Emptiness, he replies.

Coincidental meanings could collide and create new sense as they speed beyond light. Stars are keyholes, he says. My telescope can't focus.

Such a light touch: dawn on the horizon. Natural miracle of luminous skin, the magic of response: early prayers. The world reflected in a mirror, eyes reflected in eyes.

Outside the church bells peel the rising sun.

A basket of tomatoes is a rhapsody, as is a gathering of kalamata, a conspiracy of peppers and the soul of bread. Do not forget the singing wine, Yannis says.

Loving the beautiful is necessary in the village of psalms. Roses and walls cling to each other amidst the brazen display of geraniums on a blanched windowsill.

Yannis reveals his codes, certain in the knowledge only his comrades will read.

Follow the word, he says, and it will tell you what to write next. And there, in front of you, is the blank page.

The conversation circles till dusk and then we lay plans. How distant are we from walking? How many words before peace?

We are exhausted. We are alone. We climb the same hill. At the summit we find the future, then we descend once again, as in the past.

He can speak because of what he's done. Even when he greets the morning he means it.

Water is good but not for drowning sorrows. Depth of voice may not indicate depth of purpose. Eyes may betray as easily as hold.

The daily split fingernail: something new to navigate. What about old dogs?

Later, he says we don't have enough words to speak of nothing; this is on a night when lanterns lit the harbour and the boats lay silted.

Once I finished reading, the mountain stood before me higher than any mountain I'd ever seen before. And then cloud hid the peak.

A little later and it's never, Yannis says. A stray black dog stares at the vacancy, seeing what no one wants to see.

I swot at a moth bothering my left ear; I take care not to kill. The moth flutters away only to brush against my candle flame. How many charred memories?

The porch releases the day's heat. We sit, not daring to move in case we vanish. Even the nightingales cease singing, although, we're not certain whether they even began.

An old man with a silver cane passes, stumbling from memory to memory in no particular order. He is at the gate. He waves. We wave back as we always do.

Secret signals shine light years away, Yannis says, waiting for night.

The order of the sacraments has been disturbed. We have no answers.

The east wind wafts through the empty square where the Abbey once stood.

A muddy track rambles to a village of tuneless accordions; we were happy there.

Quiet; look out the window at the western river. A clock has been drowned. Many suspects roam free on the other side.

Wait for me at the tavern, Yannis says, attempting to reorder life.

His comrades disappear along with their vision, their dreams besmirched by a permanent grey stain.

What lies have been told, Yannis asks as he polishes the butt of his rifle?

Silently he walks the hall of his memory until he finds the door to an empty room.

As he enters the darkness he hears faint breathing, his own, or another?

The night is late.

Doors in Prague

Go and open the door.
Even if there's only
the darkness ticking,
even if there's only
the hollow wind,
even if nothing
is there,
go and open the door.

– **Miroslav Holub**

Enter the gallery of time, slip back, stand straight and view the past. See the beauty of spring, trampled lilacs, forgotten days of insurrection: these streets, that time and then.

Remember, the Golem sleeps in the rafters of our dream.

Ashes of the unsaid, ashes of the said don't matter when you're gone. Whatever happened we knew would happen eventually, the radio voices told us so.

At the sound of the tone it is 5.30 a.m.

Sword and shield, shield and sword, these are endless images back to genesis.

Everything is genesis for those who have read the word.

The flood comes after us whereas our scriptures advised it came well before. From where we're standing, knee deep in water, the deluge is now.

The woman in beige holds her head and sobs for fifty years at least.

The scientist speaks in forbidden words of equal measure.

Another woman, another hand pressed to mouth as the crinkled crowd surge to their fall.

Every confrontation a game someone loses while the other is lost.

Over in the baroque corner the choir still sing, even though this is against the law.

Pilsner is on tap and is that what we should be grateful for or perhaps a sip of slivovitz will do. Up to you my friend as we're all toast, we're burnt and dry.

Time is running out we know but then that's the way time goes.

What is   what ought to be
            between the two
                        infinity

In the food queue waiting ... waiting ... waiting, eyes wide full of hidden tears.

Look at us as we look at you, this crowd waiting ... waiting; for what are we waiting: The chance not to wait.

A summer day, yet we all are chilled not by the weather but by our situation.

Days of cold war and no one asked to be here.

We have no certainty, that at least is certain.

Failure is around every corner, success stole away to have a lager.

A sad man with glasses staring into space – the space that has been left by hope. A woman passes, one fake pearl earring pierced, mottled blonde hair: unknown.

They have never seen the sun.

Everyone a vagabond in their own home.
Everyone a wanderer lying in their bed.

The ruins enclose and in the next room questions are asked and people betray.

Sharp beginning of the soft world, hands to face, face to hands: To be is to fail.

Certainty of fear, the fear of uncertainty grips the politic. After thinking all will be well, after thinking all could be better, they walk the streets bereft.

Rain splatters and everyone looks at each other. Endless days are only as long as they are. Only as long as the minutes they endure.

In a town full of smoke strange days continue. And the drummer keeps the tempo and the singer quakes the song.

A young man with dark rimmed glasses holds onto his ambiguity.

Friends, listen only to official information. Lies are commonplace

Maybe they grow tired of demonstrating their failure, their inability to overcome the fact of their defeat.

Then, in a cold moment, a young body shattered. Never having a chance to see history play. A white shirt, a white face blood caked.

And beside him, barely visible, another saint prone. Is it for this moment their life unfolds?

Show your ticket, show your pass; no one enters here unless they are known.

The darkness resembles blindness sometimes.

Six o'clock and people stand about doing nothing; airing lungs.

To tweet, to tweet, sing the birds.

The summer of love lives elsewhere.

He fights for breath amidst the crowd. What is the air he's seeking? The breath he wants is ordinary that which comes from the Bohemian Sea.

And the oaks will filter impurity and all is clear. To breathe, to have lungs full of the colourless, odourless breeze.

They watch the square, stare as if there is something to see. Everyone is casual yet taut.

The motorcycle riders ready to run, but where will they go? Down to the river to drown their sorrow.

The angels of tomorrow soar on fragile wings.

His door flew open, his study gaped wide, a dark wooden door, early century solid and sure. They barged in, surrounded him at his desk, one a hero of labour, the other, languid as the day.

Don't talk; do not speak in a way we cannot understand.

They understood nothing as they always do.

The lines were cut, the windows closed to block out the possibility of change.

What will you tell your children at home, Russian soldier, when they ask you why were you here?

Kiss me twice and once again.

Only armoured men give orders now. An officer certain of his position glares at the camera. This is his history the rest will be erased.

The night eternal dark like a book not written; like a slogan, empty.

How many years of exile follow the uprising
and how many people flee?

There are no figures available the statistic machine
seized up at the moment of greatest need.

In other words; nothing added up to nothing.

Once again they lapse on the bare shore landlocked
unable to swim away to paradise.

There's no one else around hold yourself close, little
pearl.

Wear and tear, wear and tears, the ripping of cloth, the burden of fear.

No need to seek because desolation is all around in this morning.

He stares at the trucks, the tanks and the guns. Nothing else for him to see. The facts scream, before withering his heart.

The photographs are fading: the chemicals are spoilt.

And on high there is a rumbling that fades into the distance like unrequited love.

This is the door to the oldest synagogue in Europe. This door entered by humanity in all guises for every purpose:

          prayer
        consolation
          escape
        communion
          arrest
      denouncement

         and love

Smoke rises from the chimney tops, prayers are silent. Let us pray.

So many Cains, so many Abels looking for God's embrace, in the cold dawn, in the dying dusk.

On the street who is who within the fire; who lights the torch; who crouches, who smashes; who dances before the Lord?

Joshua fit.

Don't go out, stay, I said. But she didn't listen. Futile to tell her anything, ask her to do anything.

Outside they will capture you and you'll be trapped. Why want nothing, I said. But this was not possible. Her eyes glistened in a new day.

She left by the window. I stood by the door smelling the stroganoff on the stove. Only potatoes left to prepare.

In the backstreet a sleek black cat shot. All is quiet.

www.ingramcontent.com/pod-product-compliance
Lightning Source LLC
Chambersburg PA
CBHW041633040426
42446CB00025B/3500